THE IMPACT OF BLACK CHURCHES
ON THE CIVIL RIGHTS MOVEMENT

BY DUCHESS HARRIS, JD, PHD
WITH MARTHA LONDON

Core Library

An Imprint of Abdo Publishing
abdobooks.com

Cover image: Many African Americans found comfort in
spiritual songs during the civil rights movement.

abdobooks.com

Published by Abdo Publishing, a division of ABDO, PO Box 398166, Minneapolis, Minnesota 55439. Copyright © 2020 by Abdo Consulting Group, Inc. International copyrights reserved in all countries. No part of this book may be reproduced in any form without written permission from the publisher. Core Library™ is a trademark and logo of Abdo Publishing.

Printed in the United States of America, North Mankato, Minnesota
092019
012020

THIS BOOK CONTAINS RECYCLED MATERIALS

Cover Photo: Afro American Newspapers/Gado/Archive Photos/Getty Images
Interior Photos: Afro American Newspapers/Gado/Archive Photos/Getty Images, 1; William A. Smith/AP Images, 5, 43; Don Cravens/The LIFE Images Collection/Getty Images, 6–7; Red Line Editorial, 9; Everett Collection/Newscom, 12, 22–23; Hulton Archive/Getty Images, 14–15; Edwin Remsberg/VWPics/AP Images, 17; Shutterstock Images, 19, 34 (right); AP Images, 28–29, 33; Malgorzata Litkowska/Shutterstock Images, 34 (left); Harry Harris/AP Images, 36–37

Editor: Maddie Spalding
Series Designer: Ryan Gale

Library of Congress Control Number: 2019942100

Publisher's Cataloging-in-Publication Data

Names: Harris, Duchess, author. | London, Martha, author.
Title: The Impact of Black Churches on the Civil Rights Movement/ by Duchess Harris and Martha London
Description: Minneapolis, Minnesota : Abdo Publishing, 2020 | Series: Freedom's promise | Includes online resources and index.
Identifiers: ISBN 9781532190780 (lib. bdg.) | ISBN 9781532176630 (ebook)
Subjects: LCSH: African Americans--Civil rights--History--20th century--Juvenile literature. | Civil rights--Religious aspects--Juvenile literature. | Race relations--Religious aspects--Christianity--Juvenile literature. | African American Spiritual churches--Juvenile literature.
Classification: DDC 323.1196073--dc23

CONTENTS

A LETTER FROM DUCHESS

I grew up in a Black church in the 1970s and 1980s. Every Sunday my family and I would go to St. Michael's in Hartford, Connecticut. As a child, my senses were taken by the sounds of the choir and the smells of the food cooking in the church basement. I always looked forward to going to church. It was like a family reunion. It was both a refuge and an oasis.

The church was also a place where I could escape racism. For hundreds of years, Black churches have provided comfort and hope. Activists often met at these churches to discuss civil rights. In Black churches, songs often have a double meaning. On the surface, church music is about salvation for one's soul. However, in Black churches, the underlying message is often about saving Black people from racism.

Please join me in learning about the history of Black churches and how they shaped the civil rights movement. The Black church in America has helped deliver freedom's promise for hundreds of years.

Duchess Harris

Civil rights activists sang freedom songs, which often had religious or spiritual messages.

THE BETHEL BOMBING

The morning of December 13, 1962, was clear and cold in Birmingham, Alabama. A group of kids and adults were cleaning Bethel Baptist Church. They were preparing for the church's annual Christmas program.

A loud explosion echoed through the church basement. Windows shattered. The floor shook. Everyone fell to the ground. A bomb had exploded. The adults led the children to the exit. Some people had wounds on their arms from the broken glass.

A father of one of the kids arrived at the church. He had been nearby and had heard

Six years before the 1962 Bethel Baptist bombing, the house of the church's leader, Fred Shuttlesworth, was bombed.

the blast. He made sure everyone inside the church made it home safely. No one was seriously hurt, but they were scared.

This was not the first time Bethel Baptist Church had been targeted. Six years earlier, another bomb had been planted in the church. It destroyed part of the church, but no one was harmed. In 1958 a bomb was discovered and removed before it exploded. People targeted the church because it was the headquarters of the Alabama Christian Movement for Human Rights (ACMHR). This group wanted to end segregation. In the South, Jim Crow laws enforced segregation. These laws separated Black people from white people. For example, Black people had to go to separate schools and churches. Buses were also segregated. Black people were required to sit in the backs of buses. The people who attacked Bethel Baptist Church supported segregation.

CHRISTIAN RELIGIOUS IDENTITIES

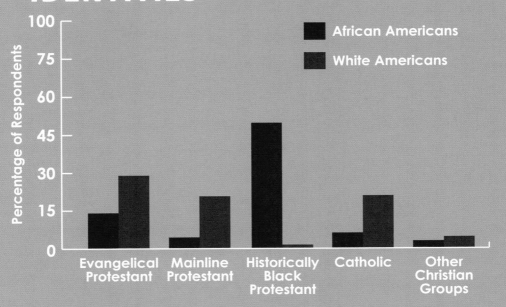

Percentage of Respondents

■ African Americans
■ White Americans

| | Evangelical Protestant | Mainline Protestant | Historically Black Protestant | Catholic | Other Christian Groups |

A 2014 survey of Americans found that approximately 80 percent of Black respondents were Christian. This graph shows some of the religious identities of Black and white respondents. Which types of Christianity did Black people identify with most? What do you think may be some reasons for the different preferences?

CIVIL RIGHTS

Bethel Baptist Church was a Black church. Its congregation was African American. They knew the bombers wanted to frighten them. But they continued to go to church. Bethel was a symbol of hope for Black people in Birmingham.

Reverend Fred Shuttlesworth led the congregation at Bethel. He was an outspoken civil rights leader. Civil rights are rights that belong to every person.

Shuttlesworth and other Black activists were part of the American civil rights movement. This was a mass protest movement. Activists asked for African Americans to be treated equally. They wanted Black people to have the same opportunities as white people. Shuttlesworth fought for integration in Birmingham. He founded the ACMHR in 1956. He was a respected leader in Birmingham's Black community.

Black churches in Birmingham were easily recognizable. Black people met regularly in these churches. Angry white people targeted the churches. They wanted to intimidate Black people. Many white people did not want to share spaces with Black people. Some attacked or even killed Black people. Bombings happened so often in Birmingham that the city became known as Bombingham.

BLACK CHURCHES

Black churches played an important role

THE ACMHR

In 1956 Alabama's attorney general shut down the state chapter of the National Association for the Advancement of Colored People (NAACP). The NAACP is a civil rights organization. After the NAACP chapter closed, Shuttlesworth created the ACMHR. The ACMHR helped with civil rights efforts. The group brought together civil rights activists in Birmingham. The activists organized civil rights demonstrations in the city.

Shuttlesworth, *foreground*, led a march to register Black voters in Selma, Alabama, in 1965.

in the civil rights movement. From the mid-1950s through the 1960s, civil rights activists held meetings at these churches. Civil rights marches often began at Black churches.

Black churches have a long history in the United States. For nearly as long as African Americans have lived in the United States, churches for African Americans have existed. Black church leaders spread messages of hope that helped people get through difficult times. Church became a safe haven for many African Americans.

Black churches are still active today. Some people think they are not as important now as they were during the civil rights movement. But Black churches are still gathering places. They continue to play a central role in Black communities.

EXPLORE ONLINE

Chapter One discusses the 1962 Bethel Baptist Church bombing and the church's role in the civil rights movement. The website below features an interview with the church's leader, Fred Shuttlesworth. As you know, every source is different. How is the information from the website the same as the information in Chapter One? What new information did you learn?

THE LIFE AND LEGACY OF FRED SHUTTLESWORTH
abdocorelibrary.com/black-churches

EARLY HISTORY

In the early 1600s, British settlers established colonies in North America. They were along the East Coast of the present-day United States. British people brought enslaved Africans to these colonies. The settlers used religion to justify slavery. They taught enslaved people their version of Christianity.

Preachers often referenced the book of Ephesians in the Christian Bible. A passage in this book says servants should obey the people they serve. Preachers avoided certain parts of the Bible that they thought went against this message. For example, there is a Bible story about how a man named Moses helped the Jewish people escape slavery in Egypt.

Dutch settlers also enslaved people. They brought 20 enslaved Africans to the colony of Jamestown, Virginia, in 1619.

15

This story is in the book of Exodus. Preachers did not share this story with enslaved people. They were afraid enslaved people would rebel if they heard it.

RELIGIOUS GATHERINGS

In the 1700s, enslaved Africans explored different Christian faiths. Many identified with the Methodist and Baptist faiths. Africans saw similarities between these worship styles and traditional African worship styles. Methodist and Baptist services often included clapping, dancing, and loud singing. The music at these services often featured African rhythms.

Spirituality was important to many enslaved Africans. It gave them hope that they would one day be free. Many white slaveholders monitored enslaved people's religious gatherings. Some did not allow enslaved people to have such gatherings. They worried that enslaved people would use these meetings to plan ways to escape.

Today, African worship styles remain popular in many Black churches.

Enslaved people who were not allowed to have religious gatherings found ways to meet secretly. They created signals or passwords. When they wanted to worship, they exchanged these signals or passwords. They met in secret locations.

In the 1800s, some Black people became preachers. Black churches became places of hope. Preachers talked about a time when Black people would no longer be enslaved.

WORSHIP STYLES

Northern and southern Black religious leaders did not always agree on how Black churches should be run. For example, Daniel Payne was an AME leader in the North. He thought dancing, drumming, and clapping were too similar to African spiritual traditions. He believed Black people should give up that style of worship. He considered quieter forms of worship to be more acceptable. But many southern Black church leaders disagreed. They wanted to keep their worship style. They believed it gave Black people hope and pride.

THE CIVIL WAR

In the mid-1800s, the United States was divided on the issue of slavery. While white southerners wanted to keep slavery legal, many northerners opposed it. This disagreement divided the country. From 1860 to 1861, 11 southern states left the Union. They formed the Confederacy. Northern states remained in the Union. Fighting broke out between the two sides in April 1861. The American Civil War (1861–1865) lasted four years. The Union won the war in April 1865. Then slavery was outlawed, and enslaved people were freed.

A statue outside a Black church in Philadelphia, Pennsylvania, honors Richard Allen. Allen was a preacher who helped form the AME church.

After the Civil War, northern Black religious leaders helped Black people in the South create churches. Two types of Methodist churches were especially popular in the South: African Methodist Episcopal (AME) and African Methodist Episcopal Zion (AMEZ) churches. The number of Black churches in the South increased between 1865 and 1900. Churches served many roles. They were places of worship, community centers, and schools.

RACIAL VIOLENCE

In the late 1800s, many white people tried to control African Americans and restrict their freedoms. Southern lawmakers created the first Jim Crow laws in the 1870s. White hate groups such as the Ku Klux Klan (KKK) formed. They attacked African Americans. When white people suspected a Black person had committed a crime, they sometimes killed the person. They also killed Black people for minor or perceived insults. These murders are called lynchings.

Many people recognized the roles of Black churches in the fight against racial violence. Black churches had a broad influence. Many Black religious leaders were well respected. People listened to them and trusted them. Some Black religious leaders spoke out against lynching.

In the early 1900s, racial violence remained widespread in the South. Many Black people left the South to escape this violence. They often settled in northern cities. They hoped to find more acceptance and job opportunities in these cities. From 1890 to 1930, 2.5 million African Americans left the South. This mass movement of people became known as the Great Migration. Migrants found comfort and familiarity in Black churches. Black religious leaders helped migrants adjust to life in the North.

PERSPECTIVES

THE ROLES OF BLACK CHURCHES

W. E. B. Du Bois was a Black writer in the late 1800s and early 1900s. In 1899 he published a book called *The Philadelphia Negro*. In it, he talked about the importance of churches in Black communities. He explained that churches had many purposes. Churches helped build Black communities. Du Bois compared churches to families. He said churches provided comfort. They also acted as authorities in communities. Black churches were like living newspapers. They helped spread information.

THE CIVIL RIGHTS MOVEMENT

I n the mid-1900s, Black churches played a central role in the American civil rights movement. Many Black church leaders became civil rights activists. In 1955 Black religious leaders planned a boycott in Montgomery, Alabama. A boycott is a refusal to do something as a form of protest. Other civil rights leaders such as Bayard Rustin helped organize the boycott too. The purpose of the boycott was to end bus segregation. Ministers spread the word to their congregations about the boycott. Many Black people stopped

Reverend Ralph D. Abernathy, *left,* **invited the Montgomery bus boycott leaders to a meeting at his church in Montgomery in 1956.**

riding buses in Montgomery. As a result, bus companies lost money. The boycott lasted more than one year. In 1956 Montgomery officials finally banned segregation on buses.

In 1957 three Black ministers helped form the Southern Christian Leadership Conference (SCLC). The leaders were Martin Luther King Jr., C. K. Steele, and Fred Shuttlesworth. They thought integration was possible without violence. They believed nonviolent protest was the best way to fight discrimination.

PERSPECTIVES
BAYARD RUSTIN

Bayard Rustin was a close friend and adviser of King. Rustin believed in the power of nonviolent protest. In 1956 he attended a meeting of the Montgomery Improvement Association (MIA). The MIA helped organize the Montgomery bus boycott. It also helped found the SCLC. After the meeting, Rustin wrote: "As I watched the people walk away, I had a feeling that no force on earth can stop this movement. It has all the elements to touch the hearts of men."

Racial violence and discrimination happened across the United States. But violence was most widespread in the South. So the SCLC focused its efforts in this region. The KKK committed much of the violence in the South. From the late 1800s through the 1960s, the KKK lynched thousands of Black people. The group was also responsible for more than 200 bombings between 1955 and 1965. The SCLC wanted this violence to end. It used churches as organizing tools. SCLC members met in Black churches. At these meetings, they spread the word about protests. One of the SCLC's main goals was to register thousands of Black people to vote. Donations from Black churches helped fund the group's voter registration drive.

DISAGREEMENTS

Not all Black churches joined the civil rights movement. Many Black religious officials feared that their churches would be targeted if they spoke out. The threat of racial violence frightened them. They did not want to put their congregations at risk. Other officials disagreed

WOMEN IN THE CHURCH

In 1819 Jarena Lee became the first Black female preacher at an AME church. She preached in Pennsylvania, New Jersey, and New York. She was also an antislavery activist. Throughout the 1900s, women continued to play important roles in Black churches. Reverend Florence Spearing Randolph preached at an AME church in New Jersey in the mid-1900s. In 1941 she delivered a memorable sermon before her congregation. She called on white people to help African Americans in their fight against racial injustice.

with civil rights leaders. They did not think protests would change the law. They thought civil rights court cases would be more effective.

The different opinions created tensions. Joseph H. Jackson was a popular reverend. He did not think protests would help Black people achieve equal rights. King disagreed with Jackson. He thought protests were important. Despite their disagreements, however, both leaders had the same goal. Both hoped to achieve racial equality.

STRAIGHT TO THE
SOURCE

Malcolm X was a civil rights leader. He was a critic of King's ideas about nonviolence. However, he recognized King's power and influence. In 1963 he wrote in a letter to King:

> *The present racial crisis in this country carries within it, powerful destructive ingredients that may soon erupt into an uncontrollable explosion. The seriousness of this situation demands that immediate steps must be taken to solve this crucial problem, by those who have genuine concern, before the racial powder keg explodes. . . .*
>
> *It is a disgrace for Negro leaders not to be able to submerge our "minor" differences in order to seek a common solution to a common problem.*

Source: "Letter to Martin Luther King Jr., 31 July 1963." *The Martin Luther King, Jr. Research and Education Institute.* Stanford University, n.d. Web. Accessed September 20, 2019.

What's the Big Idea?

Take a close look at this passage. Why did Malcolm X think it was important for civil rights leaders to work together despite their differences? What does this passage tell you about his beliefs?

PROTESTS AND GATHERINGS

On August 28, 1963, a major civil rights march took place in Washington, DC. It was called the March on Washington for Jobs and Freedom. Approximately 250,000 people participated. Among them were many religious leaders. King had helped organize the march.

The marchers began at the Washington Monument. They walked hand in hand. Many people carried signs that asked for equal rights and an end to discrimination.

The marchers stopped when they reached the Lincoln Memorial. Some activists sang

Many different people participated in the 1963 March on Washington, including Black and white religious leaders.

THE 1963 DETROIT PROTEST

C. L. Franklin was the father of singer Aretha Franklin. He was a Baptist minister in Detroit, Michigan. He led the congregation at New Bethel Baptist Church. He was also a civil rights leader and a friend of King. In 1963 Franklin and King organized a civil rights march in Detroit. The march was held on June 23, 1963. Approximately 125,000 people participated. King gave an uplifting speech in Detroit after the march.

"We Shall Overcome." This gospel song gave people hope. Some performers sang spiritual songs too. For example, Black singer Mahalia Jackson sang "I've Been 'Buked and I've Been Scorned." This song is about how faith can help people through difficult times.

Activists gave speeches outside the memorial. They also sang and led prayers. King gave his famous "I Have a Dream" speech. He imagined a future without racial discrimination. Other activists also spoke to the marchers. Some of the speakers were old. Others were young. Some speakers were religious, while others were not. The goal was to have many different voices come together. The marchers wanted to show political leaders that they were unified.

THE SIXTEENTH STREET BAPTIST BOMBING

Black activists regularly gathered in churches for civil rights meetings. Churches were often centrally located in Black communities. Many Black people attended church. It was easy to spread and learn information through churches.

PERSPECTIVES
THE FREEDOM RIDERS

By the early 1960s, the US Supreme Court had banned segregation on buses and at bus stops. In 1961 a group of Black and white activists tested these rulings. These activists called themselves the Freedom Riders. Some were religious leaders. The activists were part of a civil rights group called the Congress of Racial Equality (CORE). CORE organized a bus trip through the South. Rabbi Israel Dresner was a Freedom Rider. In a 2011 interview, he said, "The Freedom Rides were trying to say to America: we are a diverse country—let's act like a diverse country."

As landmarks, Black churches became targets. Members of the KKK often called Black churches and threatened to bomb them. The KKK hoped these threats would stop activists from meeting in churches. Some people followed through on these threats. Less than three weeks after the March on Washington, KKK members planted a bomb under the steps of the Sixteenth Street Baptist Church. Civil rights activists regularly met in this Birmingham church. The church also served as the starting point for many protest marches.

The explosion at the Sixteenth Street Baptist Church killed four young girls. A public funeral was held for three of the girls. More than 8,000 people attended the funeral. Among them were 800 religious leaders. King spoke at the funeral.

THE SELMA MARCH

Black churches became symbols of the civil rights movement. They were places of safety and hope. If marches turned violent, churches became safe houses.

Reverend John Cross, leader of the Sixteenth Street Baptist Church, observes the damage to the church after the 1963 bombing.

Activists took refuge in them. Sometimes churches even served as hospitals.

In 1965 the SCLC helped organize a 54-mile (86-km) march from Selma, Alabama, to Montgomery. Marchers protested voting restrictions. In Selma, very few African Americans could vote. They had to pass difficult tests in order to register to vote. White people did not have to take these tests.

The marchers gathered at Brown Chapel AME Church on March 7, 1965. Malcolm X and other civil

HISTORIC BLACK CHURCHES

1790

The First African Baptist Church in Savannah, GA, is founded. It is one of the oldest Black churches in the United States.

1877

The Dexter Avenue King Memorial Baptist Church in Montgomery, AL, is founded. King later preached at this church.

1908

The Brown Chapel AME Church in Selma, AL, is founded. It later served as the gathering place for the 1965 Selma March.

1926

The Bethel Baptist Church in Birmingham, AL, is founded. Shuttlesworth later preached at this church.

This timeline lists some historic Black churches and the years they were founded. Does this timeline help you better understand the influence of Black churches across generations? Why or why not?

rights activists gave inspiring speeches. The marchers prayed for strength. The leaders of the march urged people to remain nonviolent. If the police attacked them, the leaders encouraged the marchers to sit and pray in response.

The marchers sang hymns as they walked. They marched six blocks to the Edmund Pettus Bridge before they were stopped. Police and angry white people stood in the road. They chased the marchers back to the church. They hit Black people with clubs. Many people were hurt. But they could not get to a hospital because police had blocked the roads. Brown Chapel became a clinic until the police finally left. Because of the violence of this event, it became known as Bloody Sunday.

Activists did not give up after Bloody Sunday. On March 21, they attempted the march again. King led thousands of protesters on the march. They reached Montgomery on March 25.

FURTHER EVIDENCE

Chapter Three describes the Selma marches. What is one of the main points of this chapter? What evidence supports this point? The website at the link below also discusses these civil rights marches. Find a quote on this website that supports the main point. Does the quote support an existing piece of evidence in the chapter? Or does it offer a new piece of evidence?

THE SELMA-TO-MONTGOMERY MARCHES
abdocorelibrary.com/black-churches

LEGACY

The Selma marches and other protests made more people aware of racial injustices. Activists pressured lawmakers to create civil rights laws. In 1964 Congress passed a law called the Civil Rights Act. This act banned employment discrimination. Then in 1965, Congress passed the Voting Rights Act. This act outlawed obstacles that kept Black people from voting.

Despite this progress, civil rights leaders were still under threat. Even within some Black communities, conflicts arose. In 1965 shooters killed Malcolm X while he was giving a speech in New York City. Then on April 4, 1968, another tragedy occurred. A white man shot

In the 1960s, many civil rights activists protested school segregation.

and killed King in Memphis, Tennessee. King's death spurred lawmakers to take action. President Lyndon B. Johnson urged Congress to pass the Fair Housing Act. King had been one of the strongest supporters of this act. On April 11, Congress passed the act. The Fair Housing Act outlawed housing discrimination.

Throughout the late 1900s, Black activists continued to work toward equality. For example, Jesse Jackson founded Operation People United to Save Humanity (Operation PUSH) in 1971. Jackson is a Baptist minister and civil rights activist. He worked with the SCLC in the 1960s.

PERSPECTIVES

JOHN LEWIS

John Lewis was a Black civil rights activist in the 1960s. He later became a US congressman. He gave an interview in 1973. The interviewer asked if Black churches were less important than they had been in the 1960s. Lewis said, "I don't think so because the church is still one of the base areas; something that is organized. It is visible. And the Church does have a strong hold on the Black community, particularly in the South."

One of Operation PUSH's goals was to improve working conditions for Black people in Chicago, Illinois. Jackson continued his activism in the following decades. He organized a voter registration drive in Chicago in 1983.

BLACK CHURCHES TODAY

Today, some historic Black churches are still standing. Many of them played important roles in the civil rights movement. But some people think Black churches are not as influential today as they were in the 1900s.

Racial discrimination and violence are still issues today. For example, George Zimmerman shot and killed 17-year-old Trayvon Martin in Florida in 2012. Trayvon was an unarmed Black teenager. Zimmerman was in a neighborhood watch group. He shot Trayvon because he thought the boy looked suspicious.

After Trayvon's murder, some Black religious leaders organized protests. Bishop Charles Blake organized a protest rally at his church in Los Angeles, California. Trayvon's family took part.

In 2013 Zimmerman was found not guilty. Many people were outraged by this decision. Reverend Arthur Jackson III led the church that Trayvon had attended. He called for a change in the justice system. Three Black women started a movement called Black Lives Matter (BLM). BLM activists raise awareness of violence against Black people.

THE CHARLESTON CHURCH SHOOTING

In 2015 a white man walked into Mother Emanuel AME Church. This is a church in Charleston, South Carolina. The man carried a gun. He shot at the crowd of people in the church. He killed nine people. The shooter targeted Mother Emanuel because it is a Black church. He held strong racist beliefs.

Many other Black religious leaders have also spoken out against racial violence. The conversation about the role of Black churches in activist movements is ongoing. These communities have the power to bring people together.

STRAIGHT TO THE
SOURCE

Al Sharpton was a reverend during the civil rights movement. In a 2018 interview, he described his civil rights experiences. He also explained how 1960s activist movements were similar to modern activist movements:

> [Reverends William Jones and Jesse Jackson] kind of mentored me. . . . [When I was 13], Dr. King was killed, and I've been in [ministry] ever since; so I literally grew up in the ministry, and in civil rights.
>
> I think that [today] we've seen a lot of energy and activism, and some of the same . . . ways of expressing it now that you saw then. . . . Today, you have everything from civil rights guys like me, to Black Lives Matter. . . . So it's, in many ways, the same thing.

Source: Anastasia Lacina. "Civil Rights, Then and Now: A Conversation with Rev. Al Sharpton." *Fordham Political Review*. Fordham Political Review, March 9, 2018. Web. Accessed August 9, 2019.

Consider Your Audience

Adapt this passage for a different audience, such as your friends. Write a blog post conveying this same information for the new audience. How does your post differ from the original text and why?

FAST FACTS

- In the 1600s and 1700s, white slaveholders used Christianity to justify slavery. Over time, enslaved African Americans used church teachings as motivation and hope for freedom.

- Black churches were the center of many African American communities through the 1960s. They played a major role in the civil rights movement. Activists organized civil rights meetings at churches.

- White hate groups such as the KKK targeted Black churches. They wanted to discourage Black people from fighting for civil rights.

- Black religious leaders helped organize civil rights protests such as the 1963 March on Washington. Many also participated in protests.

- In 1963 members of the KKK placed a bomb in the Sixteenth Street Baptist Church in Birmingham, Alabama. The explosion killed four Black girls.

- In 2012 George Zimmerman killed 17-year-old Black teenager Trayvon Martin. Zimmerman was found not guilty. The Black Lives Matter movement was formed in response. BLM activists protest racial violence. Today, many Black religious leaders also speak out against racial violence.

STOP AND
THINK

Surprise Me

Chapter Three discusses some of the major protests of the civil rights movement. After reading this book, what two or three facts about the civil rights movement did you find most surprising? Write a few sentences about each fact. Why did you find each fact surprising?

Dig Deeper

After reading this book, what questions do you still have about Black churches? With an adult's help, find a few reliable sources that can help you answer your questions. Write a paragraph about what you learned.

Take a Stand

During the civil rights movement, some people thought religious leaders should be involved in protests, while others did not. Do you think religious leaders have a responsibility and a place in protest movements today? Why or why not?

GLOSSARY

colony
land owned by a faraway country or nation

congregation
a group of people who gather at a church to worship

discrimination
the act of treating people unfairly because of their race or other characteristics

integration
the process of bringing together people of different races

minister
someone who leads church services and ceremonies

oppression
the cruel and unjust treatment of a group of people

rabbi
a Jewish religious leader

reverend
a priest or minister of a Christian church

segregation
the forced separation of people based on race or other characteristics

ONLINE RESOURCES

To learn more about the impact of Black churches on the civil rights movement, visit our free resource websites below.

Visit **abdocorelibrary.com** or scan this QR code for free Common Core resources for teachers and students, including vetted activities, multimedia, and booklinks, for deeper subject comprehension.

Visit **abdobooklinks.com** or scan this QR code for free additional online weblinks for further learning. These links are routinely monitored and updated to provide the most current information available.

LEARN MORE

Harris, Duchess. *Civil Rights Sit-Ins*. Minneapolis, MN: Abdo, 2018.

Terp, Gail. *Nonviolent Resistance in the Civil Rights Movement*. Minneapolis, MN: Abdo, 2016.

ABOUT THE
AUTHORS

Duchess Harris, JD, PhD

Dr. Harris is a professor of American Studies at Macalester College and curator of the Duchess Harris Collection of ABDO books. She is also the coauthor of the titles in the collection, which features popular selections such as *Hidden Human Computers: The Black Women of NASA* and series including News Literacy and Being Female in America.

Before working with ABDO, Dr. Harris authored several other books on the topics of race, culture, and American history. She served as an associate editor for *Litigation News*, the American Bar Association Section of Litigation's quarterly flagship publication, and was the first editor in chief of *Law Raza*, an interactive online journal covering race and the law, published at William Mitchell College of Law. She has earned a PhD in American Studies from the University of Minnesota and a JD from William Mitchell College of Law.

Martha London

Martha London writes books for young readers full-time. When she isn't writing, you can find her hiking in the woods.

INDEX